MESSAGES FROM YANG

YOU
are the
Healing

RONNIE JACOBS

T0363626

A self-published title
Animal Dreaming Publishing
www.animaldreamingpublishing.com

MESSAGES FROM YANG
You are the Healing

A self-published title produced with the help
and support of
ANIMAL DREAMING PUBLISHING
PO Box 5203 East Lismore NSW 2480
AUSTRALIA
Phone +61 2 6622 6147
 AnimalDreamingPublishing.com
 facebook.com/AnimalDreamingPublishing

First published in 2020
Copyright text © Ronnie Jacobs

ISBN 978-0-6488436-7-2

The information in this book is intended for spiritual
and emotional guidance only. It is not intended to
replace medical advice or treatment.

Designed by Animal Dreaming Publishing

Invitation

In 1999 I arrived in Australia for the third time, and settled in Leura in the Blue Mountains, New South Wales.

One day, I came across a small shop that sold antiques and collectables. Inside, I found the tiny figure of a Chinaman, just seven centimetres tall, beautifully carved in a creamy-coloured stone. He was smiling and holding a tall staff, and beside him stood a tall crane-like bird. I instantly purchased him for two dollars and called him 'Yang.'

That evening I placed the little figure next to my bed. At just before three o'clock the following morning I awoke, my mind totally awake. I had a story to write! It was called 'Broken Bottle' and was the first of many *Messages from Yang*.

The short story had a strange title and a thought-provoking saying at the end. From then on, more messages from Yang started to present themselves, usually in the early hours of the morning. They included his tall bird TE, and a tiny green monkey called Isinka, who came on the scene later.

These short channelled, inspirational stories have many positive, gentle messages for you to enhance your life, so that you may inspire others. Perceive them in any way you choose and read them as many times as you need – consciousness is wrapped up in many different ways.

If Yang's messages help you on your journey, share them, pass them on and embrace a world of consciousness, full of love, full of messages from Yang.

For Dawn

Contents

The Broken Bottle

Yang sat and looked at the trees, their branches like long, twisting fingers reaching the Heavens. For he was counting the spaces between them. Every so often he would stop as they changed shape.

'How many spaces shall I count today?' he asked, for he was speaking to his friend TE, the bird with the silver wings and pink eyes.

TE walked to the water's edge and picked a pebble out of the lake, then placed it at his master's feet. It was the stone of a thousand colours.

Yang picked it up and held it in his hand. 'You are very wise, my friend, This stone is the colour of a thousand stones as you, my fri-end, are one of a thousand friends, as there are a thousand spaces. Thank you.' He threw the stone back into the lake. 'You have given me the answer.'

Yang studied the ripples of the water. 'Or was it the stone that gave me the answer? Or was it me, for it was I that asked TE and he fetched the stone?'

Yang scratched his head and looked up at the trees; their branches were covered with leaves the colour of green velvet. The spaces between them had gone like the ripples on the lake.

Ask of yourself, not of others

Knot of Truth

A large black cloud covered the sun, and all became dark. Yang spoke to the Heavens. 'Why do you hide your light – for it gives life and happiness?'

The cloud rumbled like thunder, sounding its discontent, but Yang had no answer. So, he spoke to TE, the bird of wisdom and gentleness. 'What is it behind the cloud that is so important to block out the sun?'

The bird picked up a leaf and placed it in his master's hands.

For a moment, Yang studied the leaf. It was magnificent in shape and colour. 'Thank you, my friend. I see the answer to my question. It is life, for life is not only behind the cloud, but it is also of the cloud itself, as is the sun. So there is no question as life cannot hide from itself.' TE flapped his wings and took off into the air. He flew high into the sky, disappearing behind the large black cloud.

His disappearance confused Yang. 'Why has my friend taken his wisdom and gentleness away?' As Yang's confusion was turning to sorrow, he felt the most gentle touch on his shoulder from behind him, for it was TE, his pink eyes full of love for his master. Yang smiled. 'And what did you find behind the cloud?' he asked.

The bird's eyes were looking towards the sky, the cloud had gone, all that remained was the sun and the colour of the sky, for it was magnificent like the leaf, like the day.

Why seek for the answer when it is in your heart

Bring Back the Flame

Yang sat on his stool outside his hut. He smiled to himself as he remembered the words of his father: 'You are the truth of the light; you are the truth of yourself.' His thoughts were interrupted by a small boy pulling at his cloak.

'Please help, old man,' he said, 'for my whole village is doomed. We have no strength left to carry on.'

Yang raised his arm in the air and with an opened hand took a handful of air. 'Here you are,' he said to the boy. 'Take this back to your village and share it with your people, for it is the essence of truth and understanding.'

The young boy looked surprised for what the old man was offering him was nothing. But he was polite and thanked Yang, then went on his way. As he sat down, Yang was joined by his friend TE. 'My friend,' he said. 'Tell me what is in the moment.'

The beautiful bird of kindness and understanding stared at his master, then very gently took a feather from his body and placed it in his master's beard. It was silver like the colour of the lake. At the same time, he took one of his master's white hairs; it shone like magic in the setting sun. TE then tucked the hair amongst his feathers.

Yang touched his friend with the middle finger of his left hand. 'Thank you, my friend,' he said, 'you have shown me that love is in the moment.'

The large bird flapped its wings and took to the sky.

Yang marvelled at how TE's body shone like a diamond in the sky. As he sat back down, Yang found a shell at his door.

On it were the words: 'Thank you for your truth and understanding. Our strength has returned – we will carry on.'

Yang laughed, and as he did, the feather flew up in the air, chasing the moment, chasing the day.

Show the way, be the way

Seeing the Way

Yang sat next to the lake. He caught sight of his reflection in the water. 'And what is your wisdom today?' he asked. As he stared into the crystal-clear water, a large, white fish with turquoise eyes raised its head to the surface. Yang felt its sadness. 'Why do you look so crestfallen, like a dark cloud?'

The fish swam closer. As it did Yang could see that it had a hook caught in its mouth. 'I see, my friend. I see your sadness.' So, Yang gently lifted the fish out of the water and held it in his hands. Its energy was both calm and serene for it trusted Yang. Using the first finger of his left hand, Yang extracted the hook and placed it on a rock. Then he gently put the fish back in the water. He returned to his hut and slept.

When Yang awoke, he sat up and was concerned that while sleeping he wasn't able to attend to the important issues of life. Then he remembered the words of his father: 'Sleep is reflection, reflection is the essence of understanding – understanding that you, as everyone else, is here for the greater reason. That reason is to give love – to be love.'

When he opened the door to his hut, a large shell was at his feet. It was full of Fu, a very rare food plant found at the bottom of the lake. Yang scratched his head and looked towards the lake. 'I see,' he said to himself. 'So your wisdom is that of gratitude.'

TE, standing next to the mandarin tree, smiled with his eyes, and using his long beak wrote the word 'love' in the sand.

A tear came to Yang's eye, for he not only realised that the wisdom of the lake was love, but that also TE and himself were love – in fact everything was love. As Yang said a prayer, the hook had melted in the sun; it was never seen again.

Look no further than yourself

Paper Raindrops

Yang spoke to his friend, TE, the bird with the silver wings and the eyes of love. 'For I must go to my brother,' he said. 'I have been called. He is sick and it is his time.' He blessed his friend by placing his hand on the bird's forehead. 'Be silent like the moment, be harmony like the day and be the happiness of a thousand hearts.' For all was silent when they parted, for all was one.

The old man with the white beard walked for nine days and nine nights, only stopping to eat from the mandarin tree and drink from the stream.

As he approached his brother's house, he was met by Fenju, his brother's wife. 'So soon you have returned,' she said. 'For only yesterday I felt you here to see your brother's soul pass on.'

Yang smiled. As he did, she passed him a small wooden box. 'Your brother wanted you to have this,' she said. Yang gave her the stone of truth and goodness, so she would live the rest of her life in harmony. They both parted.

Yang's journey back encountered anger, sadness and evil. When he arrived back at his hut, he had learnt compassion, kindness and tenderness. Smiling, he greeted his friend TE, the bird of truth and courage. He was glad to have the animal's presence about him. 'TE, you are my energy, I am your energy, together we are one.'

Yang sat down on a stool. 'I will rest my bones and other parts of my body and give them time to catch up with the energy that is in my heart.' From his bag, he took out the little wooden box given to him by Fenju. Inside was a silver feather. 'Thank you,' Yang said to TE, but the tall bird had gone, his silver wings taking him high above the clouds, above the Heavens where souls pass on.

Friendship has no words

Trees that Smile

Yang had just finished collecting wood when a traveller came by. 'Tell me, old man,' the traveller said. 'What's in the silence?.'

'How many words shall I answer your question with?'

'One,' replied the man.

Yang stared into the eyes of TE, his friend, the bird of happiness and feeling. 'You,' said Yang. 'That is the word.'

The man laughed. 'But how can I be in the silence, for I am here speaking to you, asking the question?'

'So, what are you?' asked Yang.

Again, the man laughed. 'I am a man well-travelled. I have knowledge and wisdom.'

'Thank you,' replied Yang, 'for I know what you have done – tell me what you are?'

The man scratched his beard. 'I don't know,' he replied. 'I don't know what I am.'

Yang looked at TE who walked to the traveller's side. 'Meet my friend. He is called TE, spirit of truth.'

The man laid his hand on the bird's head. 'Your friend has beauty. Not only in his eyes but also in his heart, for I feel that he is part of me as I am part of you.'

'And what is that part?' Yang asked.

The man thought. 'Is it love?' he asked. 'Is it?'

'Yes, it is,' Yang said. 'It is love. You are the love my friend –look around you, everything you see is love, love is even in the silence.'

The traveller thanked Yang, then went on his way.

Yang lit a fire and as he did the sun came up. He looked at his friend TE for they were greeting a new day in silence.

Believe in yourself. Believe in love.

Footsteps on the Water

A man went to see Yang. 'Old man, 'I feel full of anger and hate for my brother. I want to kill him.'

Yang asked him to sit down under the shade of the mandarin tree. 'Tell me,' Yang asked, 'for what reason do you have in your heart to want to kill your brother?'

The man's eyes followed a small beetle as it crossed his space. 'A year ago I gave my brother six cows. We agreed that when they were fat, he would sell them at a good price then give me half of the money. My brother is stupid because he gave the cows away. Now he is poor; now he has nothing.'

'So why do you want to kill him?' asked Yang. The man clenched his fists. 'Because he has been so stupid! Now the whole village will believe our family to be stupid, so for the honour of the family I must kill him.'

Yang stared into the man's eyes. 'So how many cows do you have now?'

'Ten,' the man replied.

'And what do they give you?' asked Yang, still looking into the man's eyes.

'They give me status and wealth.'

'And your family – what do they give you?'

The young man thought for a while. 'Well they give me happiness, kindness – everything I suppose.'

'So, give me one word for that everything,' Yang requested.

'Well, love,' the man replied. 'Love.'

'And does your family include your brother?'

'Of course it does,' the man replied with a snigger.

'So.' Yang spoke softly. 'Now you want to kill someone that gives you love?'

'Well.' The man coughed. 'I don't want to actually *kill* my brother, I am just angry with him.'

'So, does your heart still love him?' Yang asked.

The man buried his face in his hands. 'Yes.'

'And why?' asked Yang. 'Because ... because he still loves me.'

Yang stood up and walked into the sunshine. 'So, you have ten cows. So, you love your brother. So, what are you going to do?'

The man reached up and plucked a ripe mandarin from the tree and joined Yang in the sunshine. 'I'm going to give my brother five cows tomorrow for himself, because—'

Yang stopped the man. 'There is no because.' Yang smiled.

The young man returned to his village.

Yang sat and watched a dark cloud melt into the Heavens until all that was left was a sunset of love.

Speak and do what's in your heart

Fill my Cup with Moments

Yang stood in the marketplace. It was busy and noisy. He was telling some children the story of the fish and the rainbow.

A woman approached him. 'Yang, may I speak with you?' she asked.

'You are,' Yang replied, sending the children away with a little magic in their lives.

'My husband doesn't love me and I am sad.'

For a moment Yang looked into the sky as he watched the dreams from last night melt in the morning sun. 'And what is me?' he asked the woman.

She thought for a moment. 'I am a good wife. I can cook bread and keep a clean house. I tend to my children and dig the garden.'

Yang took her hands and placed them on her heart. 'So, what is me?' he asked again.

The woman searched her soul. 'Me is compassionate, loving, kind and gentle.'

'And who do you love?' asked Yang.

'I love my husband and my children.'

Yang placed his hands on his heart. 'And who do you love?' he asked again.

The woman lowered her head. 'I love myself?' she asked.

Yang lifted her head to meet her eyes. 'To love others is to love ourselves. You have the questions and the answers, now go back to your husband.'

Soon the children returned. 'Today I am catching the laughter,' he told them. 'Come join me and the butterflies.'

Their happiness could be felt throughout the market.

Two days later, Yang and TE were sitting next to the lake. The large bird with the pink eyes was showing his master how he could be love without moving a feather.

The woman from the marketplace approached with her husband. He placed a basket of fresh figs at Yang's feet; they were decorated with the flowers from the jasmine tree.

'Thank you,' the man said, 'for I love myself as I do my wife, brother and sister.'

The woman was silent.

When they had left, Yang gazed into the clear water of the lake. The white fish with the turquoise eyes was smiling at him. Just then a rainbow of a thousand colours reached across the sky and touched them both.

Walk your talk

Butterflies Can

A healing woman came to see Yang. 'I hear that you are full of wisdom and understanding,' she said, 'and that you are a diamond amongst a sea of pearls.'

'And what do you hear in between – in between the darkness and the light?'

'I have come because I can no longer heal. Once, many people visited me. From sickness I gave them health. Now I am empty. I have lost the healing.'

Yang walked into his hut. He returned with a small wooden box. He gave it to the woman. 'During the day place this box outside your hut. The music from it will become your healing, and at night let its chimes flow with the stars.'

The woman thanked him, then left.

Yang sat and looked at the lake. 'How beautiful you are,' he said. 'How serene.' Its reflection was that of everything, for all is oneness. A small monkey came and sat next to Yang. It had green eyes and a pink nose. Yang took from his bag a flute and it started to dance. It jumped up and down, its energy was that of complete happiness, unconditional love. When Yang had stopped playing, he fed his little friend some nuts and fruit.

A man's voice made Yang look up. 'So, you have found my monkey,' he said. 'I am taking him to the market to sell him, he is no good to me, he is as deaf as the earth.'

Yang stood up. 'Sell him to the one with the colour of love and you will get a good price.'

It was sometime later when the night sky became a blanket of stars that Yang returned to his hut. The small monkey with the green eyes and pink nose sat on his shoulder. 'I shall call you Isinka, spirit of joy,' he said. The tiny creature reached over and put one of his fingers up the old man's nose. It was the monkey's sign of affection.

About this time, buds started to open and small flowers appeared. Bees and other insects investigated each on their own, for they were spreading their magic across the world. Time seemed to stand still and yet it shifted slowly like clouds, like the water of the lake, like the smile of the day.

'My dreams are so wonderful,' Yang said, as he opened his eyes. A small monkey head popped up from under Yang's beard and for a brief moment both Master and friend were as one at the beginning of a new day.

Yang was eating fresh figs when the healing woman approached. 'I bring you the surrender of my heart,' she said. 'My healing has returned.' Yang smiled as she placed the music box on a log. 'You were right,' she said. 'The music from the box became the day and the night. Now, more than many visit.'

He took the box and gave it back to her. 'Take it, for now it is your friend.'

The healing woman accepted it back and opened it. 'But it's empty,' she said. 'But where did the music—'

Yang stopped her words. 'You are the music —
as you are the healing.'

You have done nothing wrong

Silence of the Sky

A misfit came to see Yang. 'I have decided to end my life now,' he said. 'And why do you choose Heaven so soon?' asked Yang, sitting down on a small stool with Isinka his monkey friend.

The misfit started to cry. 'Nobody loves me because I have been born small and out of shape.'

Yang leaned back so Isinka could snuggle into his beard. Isinka liked it there because it was warm and close to his master's heart. Yang spoke softly, his words were of compassion and kindness. 'When the day becomes long, meet me in the marketplace, and bring with you no fear or sadness, for all will be well.'

The misfit left.

Later, when the butterflies had enjoyed their time together, Yang stood in the marketplace with the misfit. People gathered around them, some laughed, some scorned, others were silent.

A man threw a stone, it hit the misfit. As he went to throw another, Yang nodded his head just once. Instantly he and the misfit were surrounded by children. It was as if they had come from nowhere. They chatted. They embraced Yang and the misfit.

The man laughed out loud. 'You old fool,' he said. 'So now you can do tricks?'

Instantly all the children clapped their hands and suddenly a thousand doves flew across the sky. The crowd were in wonder at the magical sight above their heads.

'And is your stone a trick?' Yang asked, as the man found that he was now holding a mandarin in his hand.

In a moment the doves had gone to their place of rest. The man held his head in shame. He went to speak but as he did the misfit stood before him with his arms out. They embraced.

Messages from Yang

The man was in tears. Others around became the sadness.

Yang, his voice pure as the day, sang these words. 'You are the love that's in your heart, you are the love from the start. Embrace each other every day. No-one can take your love away.'

The children laughed, people joined in. For a moment, the marketplace was the joyous colour of love.

That evening Yang wrote: 'Love is a tornado. We are taken by it, we feel shaken like a ship on an angry sea. Then when we understand that the ocean is within us and accept it, peace returns, and the ocean becomes a lake of serenity. The love within us and the universe flows freely.'

Soon the sky became a multitude of stars all on their own journeys. Yang sat next to the fire, TE meditating not far away. Yang spoke to Isinka next to him. 'And what is tomorrow my little friend, for what shall the essence of the day bring us?'

For a moment Isinka thought, then turned around showing his bottom to his master. It was the little monkey's way of telling Yang that he had no idea about tomorrow.

Yang laughed out loud. His laughter could be heard in the Heavens.

TE opened one eye. 'What happiness that laughter is,' he thought.

Isinka snuggled into Yang's beard. He was just about to wonder, when the rhythm of his master's heart sent him to sleep.

Attachment - Separation - Connection

Faces left Behind

Yang spoke to a fisherman. 'How's your catch?' he asked. The fisherman tapp-ed his clay pipe out on a large rock and shook his head. 'I am fed up. There are no more fish left in the lake. I'll never catch anything ever again. It doesn't matter what bait I use – no fish come my way.'

Yang pointed to a fly buzzing about. 'See that fly,' he said. 'I've caught that fly.'

The fisherman laughed. 'But how have you caught it for it buzzes around our heads?' The man blinked, just once. He missed the old man's move.

Yang opened his hand in front of the man's eyes. The fly flew away from his palm.

'But how did you do that?'

Yang smiled. 'How many fish have you caught tomorrow?'

The fisherman looked blank and lit his pipe.

Yang repeated, 'How many fish have you caught tomorrow?'

'Ten,' replied the fisherman.

'Then leave early and take no bait – just your net.'

The fisherman walked away with a look of bewilderment, a feeling of hope and the satisfaction of a full pipe.

The day passed into the night, eyes closed with sleep, and souls played their own music. Morning brought grey skies. Yang watched TE play with the wind, his silver body contrasting like a dancing crystal.

Later Yang picked a basket of walnuts and placed them outside his hut. It was at that time when he heard his name – it was the fisherman walking towards him. His clay pipe was sticking out the side of his straw hat. 'It must be there for safe keeping,' thought Yang.

'Thank you,' the fisherman said, 'for today I caught ten fish with no bait. It's amazing and you are also amazing.'

Yang replied, 'As is the time between today and tomorrow, as was the fly that buzzed around our heads.'

The fisherman laughed out loud, for he was laughing into thin air, as Yang had gone, except that is, for the smile he left in the sand.

Start with faith

Dogs are our Teachers

A warrior passed by Yang's hut. 'Old man!' he shouted. 'Give me a drink for I am on a conquest.'

The water from Yang's bucket was as clear as crystal as he filled a shell and gave it to the man. 'And what is your conquest?' asked Yang.

The warrior threw the shell in the air and stuck out his chest. 'I am the finest warrior in the land,' he said. 'I am a master with the sword and spear – no man has ever beaten me. I have power stronger than that of the sea.'

'So, what is your conquest?' Yang asked again.

'To be the greatest warrior there is.'

'But aren't you that already?'

The warrior digested his words. 'I see that you are clever, old man. Clever with words and wisdom, and yet it is my belief that I am the first real warrior that you have ever met. Maybe I should show you how to treat me with respect.'

Yang took from his belt a small purse. He opened it and threw a round silver disc on the ground. On it was the Black Star. Its reflection caught the man's eye.

'Ha ha, the Black Star, the sign of the Master of Masters. I have seen many of them, old man, many fakes.' Although the warrior had his eyes on Yang, he didn't see him move, just felt a light tap behind his ear. That's when his world turned to darkness.

Later when he awoke, the moths were playing games above his head and stars began to peep. He lay next to the fire; he was naked except for his loin cloth.

Yang sat next to him. 'Warrior. Eat the food that is placed next to you, then carry on with your conquest for you do not need your sword or armour. When you have learned what is in your heart, your realisation will be that you are the greatest spiritual warrior ever.'

After eating without a word, the warrior left. As he walked away, the shell fell from the sky and tapped him on the shoulder. He turned.

'Good luck my spiritual warrior,' Yang called. 'Good luck!'

Be

At the Centre of the Edge

TE, the bird of peace and learning sat watching his master. 'Today I want to make him very happy because it is his birthday.' He spoke to himself softly in Crane language.

Yang had finished talking to some children – they ran off laughing for he had told them the story of the butterfly and the cross-eyed frog.

The bird with the silver wings and pink eyes thought for a while. 'Maybe I shall fly high in the sky then hover endlessly above my master's head – he likes that. Or I could fly close to the lake and make patterns on the water with my wings, I know my master will like that.' It was while he wasn't thinking that TE just went and did what he felt. He collected a walnut, a

mandarin, a fig and a jasmine flower, then placed them at Yang's feet.

Yang smiled. 'Thank you, TE. You are a crane of
beauty. Thank you for your gifts.'

The large silver bird thought for a moment. He
wanted to give his master more because he
loved him so much. Soon he returned with a
small stick, a piece of string and a white stone.

Yang laughed. 'Your wisdom and understanding
– like your love – is welcome as raindrops on a
hot day. The string I will use to make a candle,
the stick I will use to scratch my back and the
white stone I will use to guide me through the
night for it is the stone of awareness.'

As the bird sat watching his master make a
candle, the sunset turned the sky into a canvas
of flame. TE watched his friends fly to their
roosts for the night. He remembered all the
things that he had given Yang for his birthday,
and as the old man finished his job, TE just went
and did what he was feeling and sat down next
to his master. He placed his long beak on Yang's
lap and closed his eyes. As he did, he felt Yang's
hand on top of his head.

'Thank you, TE. For you have given me the greatest gift of all – the gift of love.'

Taste it, feel it, be it

The Bitter Taste of Honey

One day a man came to see Yang. 'Now that you have seen me,' Yang said, 'what do you ask?'

'I have been tricked, and I feel a fool.'

Yang picked up three flat stones, then threw them across the lake, each skimming in different directions. Touching the water many times, the lake became a multitude of ripples. Yang spoke to the man. 'Have you seen a lake smiling?'

The man looked blank. 'Smiling? They are just ripples, and you couldn't have done it without the stones.'

Yang smiled. 'You mean these stones,' he said, opening his hand. 'Let's go and sit over there next to my friend TE, for he has serenity and calm around him.'

When they had sat, Yang asked the man about the trick. He told how he had traded a bag of golden seeds for a bag of jasmine tea only to find that when he got home the tea was nothing more than dried leaves from the Yini tree. 'And they are worthless to me,' he said.

'So why do you come to see me?' asked Yang.

'I see you because you are fair, you are wisdom and true. You are Yang.'

'Thank you, my friend,' Yang said, picking up from the ground a small piece of wood. 'Take this to the person who gave you the dried leaves. Tell him it's a gift and that you hold him no resentment. He will ask you what is the wood. Tell him that it comes from the Tree of Dreams.'

The man thanked Yang, then went on his way.

TE, the silver bird with pink eyes, walked up to his master.

'Hello, my friend of trust and grace, show me what's in a sign.'

The tall silver bird bent down and drew a heart with his beak in the sand.

'Thank you, my friend,' Yang said. ''Tis love that is in every sign.'

The stillness of the day melted in the darkness, eyes closed as spirits, their beauty touching the universe.

The following morning, Yang walked in the forest to find a quiet space.

The man who had been tricked approached him. 'Thank you, Yang. I now have my golden seed back, plus a goat and a duck, for I gave him the wood from the Tree of Dreams.'

Yang smiled. 'Good. Now he shall sleep a better man, and his dreams – what dreams? And what golden seeds, for isn't that jasmine tea I see in your bag?'

Nothing belongs

Sacred Heart

Yang's eyes opened. The light of the day was just showing its face, all hearts were still asleep, dreams floating with conscious intent. Isinka wasn't in his usual place under his master's beard, instead the warm night found him and TE asleep just outside Yang's hut. TE, his long legs tucked underneath him, eyes closed, possibly on some crane adventure. A tiny monkey hand showing through his feathers on his back told Yang that Isinka had found a feathered bed for the night. As they lay there together sleeping, it was a sight to behold. If there is a tear for happiness, then the old man was happy to shed a few.

Silently, Yang sorted a few things He took his staff, then walked along where mandarin trees hang low with fruit, where white doves float like paper tissues against a grey sky, and came across a man sitting on the ground.

'Help me,' the man said, 'for I am a cripple and need money.'

'Tell me why your soul chose to lose your leg?'

The man looked at Yang with resentment. 'You don't understand, old man. Now give me some money and go away.'

Yang bent down and placed his hand on the man's heart. 'Here you have everything you need. Goodness, courage, strength and love. Tell me what else do you need?'

The man started to cry. 'But why me? Why me, my leg, why?'

Yang took the man's hand and kissed it. 'My friend, you chose it as you chose your path in life. Take time to search your soul, to look within, for you will have no need to cry.' Yang blessed the man, then walked on his way.

Later that day Yang saw the man next to the lake. He was making a fishing net. Yang approached him and as he did, the cripple stood up, but he didn't speak. Yang took from his pouch a small bottle. 'These are your tears. Keep them for they are the tears of your soul. Take this pink ribbon and tie the bottle next to your bed. Pray each night, for you shall never resent again.' As Yang walked away, he whispered, 'My friend, continue to look within and your reward will be greater than any money can buy.'

As Yang walked back to his hut, the doves returned to their place of rest. They were happy that they had sprinkled goodness, courage, strength and love across the universe.

Abundance is endless

Before your very Eyes

'Excuse me sir, but can you work tricks?' Yang looked up from cooking his rice. Standing in front of him was a woman. 'I only know the trick of the light,' Yang replied. 'When a star is so bright it touches my heart, and when the sun is so golden that it makes me laugh.' He could see that his words had fallen on deaf ears. 'So, what are your words?' he asked.

'I am ugly,' she said. 'I've always been ugly, it pains my heart. When will I ever be beautiful?'

'Meet me in the marketplace when the sky turns to gold.'

The woman shifted off, mumbling to herself.

Yang ate his rice with lemongrass and ginger. TE sat under a tree, wondering how much happiness he could fit into one day. Isinka was showing his friend that there was no time to wonder when you can be the happiness now, as he was using a walnut, banging it on a rock. TE thought Isinka was happiness in action.

The marketplace was busy, peoples hearts beating like drums sending messages through the silence. Yang met the woman. In his hand he held two stones. 'Watch,' he said, as he created beautiful magic by throwing them in the air. 'You try.' He handed her the stones.

Without a word, the woman started to create amazing things with the stones. People gathered around, amazed at such wondrous fun. They laughed, they applauded, their hearts full of joy. Soon the market faded, as rainbows do.

'Did you see those people looking at you?' Yang said to her. 'Did you feel their happiness? It was the enlightenment of your soul that danced.'

'Yes, it was wonderful. I felt as if I had been touched by love.'

'That's because you are love,' Yang replied. 'You are love and love is beautiful, so go on your way and take these little stones with you, for one of them is courage and the other is the stone of you ... the stone of love.'

Behind every cloud

Secrets

Yang had been walking for some time. While he moved forward, he recalled words from his heart: 'I am of conscious self, I am the light of life, pure in spirit. Take me as I am. I am.'

As he sat next to a Yini tree he was joined by a little girl. She had dark straight hair. Her face was pale and beautiful. It reminded Yang of a very rare pearl called Tunga, Clarity of the Sea.

She reached out and touched Yang's hand, pressing her palm into his. Then using his middle finger, touched her ear and lips.

Yang realised by this that she was a deaf mute. They both stood up together. Yang took from his bag a silk scarf, then tied it around her head across her eyes, so now she was blind. Then the young girl walked with him, trusting him, because she could feel his energy of kindness, gentleness and love.

After short times they would stop, Yang offering her some things to smell – a flower or a leaf from a tree or the earth. After a while they came to the edge of the lake and sat on a large rock.

Just at that moment TE appeared. It was as if he had been waiting for them. The large bird with the pink eyes joined them at the rock. For a moment Yang and the girl sat in silence, motionless, like stillness does. Then she reached out and touched TE on the neck. He instinctively touched her with his beak, it was a connection of love. She leaned forward and hugged him. From behind her blindfold, tears ran down. The sun, the wind evaporated them, then floated away to tear-land above the Heavens. For a while they sat, in the moment of the day, accepting the love.

After a while Yang and the little girl returned to the Yini tree. There Yang spoke to his guides. After he picked a small olive plant, for it was the symbol of belief, Yang placed it on his chest. Then, holding the girl against him, after a while

Yang was able to speak to her - not through his lips, through his heart. And although she could neither hear, speak or see, she could feel the old man's love. She could understand the words from his heart. Together, like the dewdrops and the morning, they spoke to each other. She could hear Yang's voice as clear as the lake, as clear as the music of love.

Soon she left, her blindfold gone, for her eyes will find her home. In that brief moment, she smelled, tasted, experienced love. For a moment she was taken from emptiness to the fullness, from the darkness to the light, from the now to the being.

Later that evening, Yang saw her again, this time in the clouds, her clarity of consciousness peeping through like a sunflower showing its face for the first time. Yang slept well that night, his soul travelled well, tasting freedom and experiencing love.

The following day, as the sky became golden like the sun, as feathered friends shared their dreams in morning song, Yang returned to the edge of the lake and the large rock. TE, his beautiful friend, was still sitting in the exact same place as yesterday. Yang kissed his friend on the top of his head. 'Come TE,' he said. 'Let's share our secrets of love and kindness. Let's create the gentleness and the beauty of the day, so that it will hear, speak and see.'

I will rise up and taste the Me

Drums that Cry

Yang sat in his hut. He was reading the words of Sin-Ya, the Great Master: 'For thou shall move towards, but not against, and be the openness of your soul.'

Yang walked out into the sunshine. TE the bird of happiness and faith sat on a stump. 'Hallo my friend. You remind me of the space – so pure, so innocent. Take to the sky and show me your wisdom.'

TE smiled like butterflies do when they have just met, flapped his wings and lifted from the earth. Higher and higher his silver body on its journey of freedom.

Yang watched his friend fly higher until he was lost behind the clouds, frowning. 'For where are you?' he cried. 'Lost forever?' A tiny pull on his robe made him turn around. TE stood there, in his beak a leaf from the Ga tree. Yang took it for it was the symbol of wisdom. 'Now show the truth,' Yang asked.

Once again TE took to the skies. This time he flew directly above his master's head, hovering, floating, his wings perfectly still.

Yang was amazed and cried with joy. 'You truly are the essence of truth,' he shouted as he wiped away the tears from his eyes. Again, he felt a tiny pull on his robe and turned around. But TE was not there, just an empty space. 'My friend, where are ... ?' But his words floated towards the Heavens when he found his friend sitting on the stump. Yang smiled. 'You have taught me not to have expectations, not to cry like the wind. And you have reminded me of the space ... I am.'

Creation is being

Tapping In

I n the forest close to Yang's hut was a space. It was the only part where the sun filtered through the trees to the forest floor. Butterflies often played together there, creating a magical rainbow of dancing colour.

Other creatures came to the space and were joyous because the sun warmed their tiny bodies. They passed their happiness onto their friends so that the forest became a joyous place to be, and all because of one small ray of sunshine.

This is where Yang would come to connect to his soul's purpose, for it was a sacred place. Today Yang stood for a moment taking in the magic that surrounded him for it was both calm and special. He took from his bag seven small stones and set them in a circle on the forest floor. They were of truth, understanding, kindness, awareness, wisdom, gentleness and love. He then lit a candle and placed it in the middle of the circle and closed his eyes.

Soon the forest fell silent. Or, was it that this old man had reached his inner being, that of complete peace and harmony? For even the wind had respect for the flame. Yang's being followed the road towards the light. On its journey it encountered anger and resentment, ego and mistrust, and also pain and hurt. Once, at the light, Yang's self realised his 'I-amness', delighting in the truth, understanding and awareness, tasting the kindness, wisdom and gentleness, being the love. Soon the forest became awake. birds, their songs being carried by the wind. Trees embraced, branches gently touching, like love touches the heart.

Yang stood up, the seven stones had melted into dust, each energy giving itself to the universe. As he walked back to his hut, Yang thanked the forest for its harmony and gentleness, remembering the flame that he had left burning in the forest. Just then a light inside his hut caught his eye. As he entered, on the floor

before him was the candle, its flame whole-
some, in a circle around it were seven ... silver
feathers.

Sow the seed of you

Lemons and Others

Yang sat on a stool in the marketplace, between the clothmaker and the woman who reads the cards. The sound was that of drums, gently beating to the rhythm of the day – people's shoulders touching, souls mingling. Happiness was part of the rhythm, part of the mingling.

'So, now is your holiday?' he asked the woman.

'What holiday? For I work to pay for my food, my children.'

So, what would you be if you couldn't read the cards?' Yang asked.

'I'd be at home. A sorrowful sight, full of sadness and loss.'

'So, tell me about this moment.'

'I am happy, for many people come to me, they fill my cup with appreciation.'

Yang shifted from one leg to the other and stroked his beard. 'So, tell me about happiness and appreciation – does it feel like a holiday?'

The woman thought for a while. 'It feels like harmony and gladness.'

'Like … like a holiday?' asked Yang.

'Yes, like a holiday.'

'Look at your next card. It is a heart, isn't it?'

She turned over the next card and it was a heart – the heart of love – and it left behind the sorrow, sadness and the loss.

'I am a fool,' a man shouted. 'I am a fool.'

People laughed at him, some even threw sticks. Leaving the woman, Yang stood up from his stool and approached the man. 'And what is a fool?'

'I don't know anything,' he replied. 'I was born a fool and will always be a fool.'

'Do you know that you are honest?' asked Yang.

'Yes, I am very honest.'

'And do you know that the sun comes up in the morning and that to experience the light you have to know the darkness?'

'Yes,' said the man. 'All people know these things, but I am still a fool.'

Yang stopped a man passing. 'Excuse me sir, what is your trade?'

The man lifted his nose in the air. 'I am a man of the law,' he replied.

'So, you are an honest person?' Yang asked.

The man laughed. 'What is honesty?'

'And do you know the darkness?' Yang asked.

'Darkness? Can't say I do. I've never thought about it.' The man continued on his journey.

Yang turned to the man who called himself a fool. 'You know that you are honest, and yet that man didn't even know what honesty was, and the darkness, he never even thought about it. He was a man of the law, respected, learned. So, what are you?' asked Yang.

'I am his brother,' the man replied.

'As we are all brothers, as we are all one. Now walk your way, for you have experienced the light. And the fool – what fool?'

The woman with the cards stepped forward. 'Thank you, old man, for my bag is now half full of coins. Tell me – how did you know that my next card would be a heart?'

Yang smiled. 'Because you are a heart of love, just as your bag is now full of coins.'

The woman looked into her bag, her mouth fell open. 'But ... how?' She was talking to the space – the space of consciousness.

Know

The Listening Stone

Yang watched his friend Isinka walk down to the lake. The little monkey was only gone a short while, before returning with a shell, holding it in his little hands. Yang could see that his small friend had collected some water from the lake. Yang's mind was curious and felt that there was a need in the little monkey's doing.

Putting the shell down in front of TE, Isinka collected some moss, just a tiny handful, and dipped it in the water. Then, standing as high as he could in front of TE, he showed it to his friend. It was at that moment that Yang saw the sadness in the large bird's eyes. TE shook his head, for there was pain.

Yang moved closer and could see that TE's left eye was inflamed. 'My friend. The day has cast its shadow.' Yang looked closer still. 'And this shadow I cannot heal. We shall walk the way of the poppy fields and visit the healer.'

That night TE slept with his master, his long beak resting on Yang's lap. Every so often Isinka bathed his friend's eye with the wet moss, for the water from the lake was both cool and soothing.

The following morning, before the sun showed its smile, Yang and TE walked the crooked road to the poppy fields. Yang had made a sling. TE fitted in, snuggled on his master's back, his large beak resting on Yang's shoulder. Isinka would fit in one of the large pockets of his coat, but the little green monkey with the pink nose had other ideas and joined TE in the sling.

For a while TE's pain drifted away, for their connection was complete harmony, complete love. During the journey Yang sang songs of kindness, understanding and happiness. In turn TE made soft crane noises of gratitude that only his master could hear. Isinka slept in complete harmony. All were one.

It was late in the day – when the gentleness of nature sits and rests – that they arrived at the healer's place. Both men greeted each other with a sign, a word and a gift.

The healer touched TE's eye with a blue crystal, then gave Yang a small bottle of clear liquid. 'Bathe his eye each time you see the yellow butterflies tasting the nectar of the jasmine flower.'

Yang thanked the healer. Isinka gave him a small piece of dried moss for his kindness. The healer let them sleep in a small cave, it was both dry and warm. He gave Yang bread and fruit. Isinka ate, TE didn't.

The next day they walked – Yang singing, TE sleeping and Isinka playing with his master's hair. Soon days melted into each other as days do, as serene, as gentle as silence.

The yellow butterflies danced well for TE, visiting the jasmine flower on their journeys of happiness. Soon the silver bird had pink eyes that were as clear as crystal, like the water of the lake, like the Heavens above the painted sky.

Yang met the healer who was passing nearby. 'What blessing you have to heal. Tell me what was the magic in the little bottle, for it gave newness and life?'

The healer spoke no words, just pointed towards the lake, then placed his hand on Yang's heart.

Realisation

Jumping Off

Yang watched some young men in the marketplace. They were taunting a smaller, skinnier member of their group. He looked lost and scared. Yang approached them. 'Have you ever seen a golden diamond?' he asked them.

They laughed. 'There's no such thing,' the biggest of them said.

Yang pointed to the top of the hill. 'Take more than one step in that direction and you shall see a golden diamond.'

The group of young men left excited with anticipation in their hearts. Yang spoke to the one who was being taunted. 'Let them go, for all they will find is the sun, the most beautiful golden diamond of them all. You look sad.

Is your heart heavy because they taunt you?'

The young man nodded in agreement. They both sat down on a log, the sound of the marketplace around their ears, like a music box that's never ending, never ending.

Yang spoke to a passing butterfly. 'Take your colour and spread it around the world, for it is a rainbow of love, unless there is something else?'

'So, tell me,' Yang spoke to the young man. 'If you take away the sadness and heavy heart, tell me what is left?'

The young man searched for an answer, for it was while he was searching that the butterfly returned – this time landing on the back of his hand. For a moment both the young man and the small creature looked at each other, then it flew off around the world.

'So, what is left?' asked Yang again.

'Is it love?' the young man asked.

'Is it?' Yang replied. 'Your friends are coming down from the hill – I must go. And he stood up and then walked away into the shade of a temple.'

When the young men arrived back they were full of loss and resentment. 'That old man – he tricked us,' they said to the smaller, skinnier one. 'Was he your friend?' they asked.

'Yes,' the smaller man replied. 'He taught me that there is no fear, sadness or a heavy heart – and that I am love.'

The others laughed. 'Love, so what is love?' they scorned.

The young man held out his open arms. 'Come, embrace the love.'

Their faces changed from scorn to confusion, from confusion to loss, and from loss to fear. As the music box of life reached full pitch, each of them scattered, like seeds, or brains, or leaves in the wind.

Yang smiled from the shade of the temple as the most beautiful golden diamond of all lay to rest until another day.

The expectation of nothing

Song of the Rose

A man came to see Yang. He had a baby in his arms. 'I have just found this little one down by the lake, hidden behind some rocks. There is no mother, what shall I do?'

Yang took the man into his hut. The child looked cold and pale. 'I shall give it some goat's milk. It will warm it and bring happiness to itself.'

The man stood by the door. 'I must go now. I have things to do.'

Yang smiled. 'Yes, things are always doing, aren't they?' He thanked the man who left, leaving only his shadow.

Yang spoke to the tiny pink person. 'I am Yang, I am your dreams – and Isinka my little monkey friend, he is your laughter.' Then, placing his finger on the child's forehead, Yang said a prayer. Its little face lit up with a smile of happiness and serenity for something told it that there was warm goat's milk on the way.

That night Yang sang songs to this precious soul. He sang songs to himself, TE and Isinka. Moths and night creatures listened, all was wondrous and beautiful, all was one.

The following morning, Yang carried the baby to the village. Isinka came along sitting on his master's shoulder. The little monkey felt a connection with the small one.

Yang's knowing took him to a place where lost people lived, and there he found the mother of the child. 'No, I do not want it, I do not love it. It has bought shame on my family.'

'And what is shame?' asked Yang. 'Is it greater than love?'

'Go away, old man, I care not for you or the thing.' She sat on a large log hiding her face in her hands.

Yang took the child to the edge of the lake. It was wrapped well. He placed it in a round basket with a large handle, then put it on the water pushing it off gently. The gentle breeze carried into the middle of the lake. Soon the cry from the little one's lungs could be heard across the water. Small monkeys chattered, Isinka joined in their chorus, swans glided across the lake like white kites, majestic, graceful in love.

The mother ran from the place where lost people live. Others gathered. She cried the hurt from her heart. Without hesitation she walked into the water.

 Yang stopped her. 'What is it that pains your heart? Is it the shame?' Yang placed his finger over her lips. As he did, the woman felt a gentle touch behind her. Standing there was TE, the silver bird with gentleness in his heart. He was holding the basket in his beak, the baby was asleep. As she took the little one in her arms, Yang had a tear in his eye. 'Through the darkness there is always light, always love,' he said.

The woman nodded respect to Yang. As she left, he handed her a silver disc. On it was the Black Star, the highest order of Master of Masters. 'Take this and share it with your people – you will never be lost again.'

For a brief moment, the monkeys stopped chattering. Isinka was missing his little friend already. TE and Yang stood in silence, in fact the whole world became silent, silent for love.

Giving what greater gift

The Stick

Yang looked across the village square. People were gathering, their faces like grey skies: eyes of sadness, souls lost. 'Why be unhappy when the fruit of love is so sweet?' he asked as he approached.

'We are yesterday people,' a young man said. 'We must move on. The elders have told us so.'

'My eyes count at least thirty of you,' Yang said. 'And I have never seen such sadness in your eyes.'

The young man spoke again. 'The elders tell us that we are empty, our minds and bodies no use to this village, so now we must go.'

Yang pointed towards the sun. 'Wait for a while, until the golden diamond of life lowers its head to rest.'

The people agreed to wait. Yang spoke to one of them, a young boy. 'Go fetch me the elders. Tell them it is Yang.'

Soon the boy returned, behind him walked the three elders. On meeting Yang, they nodded their heads in respect.

'Tell me. What is yesterday and empty?'

The oldest and wisest elder, his voice loud, replied, 'This village has no use for these people.'

Again, Yang asked, 'What is yesterday and empty?'

Each elder was silent, for they had no answer.

Yang asked a young boy to step forward. First, he gave the lad wax to put in his ears, then using a silk scarf, covered the boy's eyes and mouth, so now he could not hear, see or speak. The boy was calm and happy because his heart loved and trusted Yang.

Yang spoke to the elders again. 'Tell me. What is your wisdom? But do not speak it.'

Each elder briefly closed their eyes, opened them, then nodded to Yang. Yang walked behind the boy, standing with his eyes closed, his hands on his heart. At that moment, the people, the market was silent. It was as if life had stood still. Then without a word, the boy walked forward towards the three elders, although he could not hear, see or speak. He walked around people, stopping in front of each elder. Then he returned to where he had been standing, in front of Yang. Yang removed the wax from the boy's ears and the silk scarf from around his head.

'Tell me,' Yang asked the boy, 'what is the wisdom of the elders?'

The lad pointed with his finger. 'That one's wisdom is stillness. That one's wisdom is learning. That one, the last one ...' The boy paused for a moment. 'That one is the stars.'

Each elder looked surprised. 'He is right,' one of them said, 'for today he is full of knowledge.'

Yang stood with the boy amongst the so-called 'empty people', his eyes meeting those of each of the elders. 'He is one of these people. Their emptiness is his fullness, their yesterday his today.'

The sky turned the colour of gold dust as the sun laid its head to rest. birds returned to their sleeping places, so they could fly in their dreams.

The oldest and wisest elder came and stood among the people and in front of Yang. 'You may all stay,' he said, in a loud voice. 'Stay for the rest of your lives, for you are the people of the moment.'

The three elders thanked Yang for his consciousness. Yang in return gave each of them a small shell for it was for their giving, acceptance and their love.

You are the healing

The Joy of Laughing

Yang sat looking at the flame of a candle, for he was enchanted by its beauty. 'Have you ever seen a happy flame?' he said to TE, his friend of harmony and patience. 'I have, because I am the flame and I am happy.'

TE stared at his master, his pink eyes reflecting the beauty of his soul. He wanted to tell Yang how much he loved him, how much he respected the old man's wisdom.

Yang stood up and placed his left hand on TE's head. 'I know, I know. Come, let's speak to the lake.' They walked from the hut. Isinka played in the mandarin tree. Yang knew that he would be happy until they returned.

At the lake Yang and TE sat in a bumboat. It was small, the shape of something round – they fitted in well. The water was calm and serene, its energy was peace and acceptance. Both Yang and TE remained still as small ripples carried them into the middle of the lake. The sky was the colour of snow above their heads, its reflection on the lake made it look like a mirror, with a thousand ripples.

Yang leaned over and put his hand in the water. Soon many fish swam around, each one taking its turn to kiss his hand. It was as if they were accepting the gift of happiness, the gift of the flame.

The large white fish with the turquoise eyes flipped itself out of the water into Yang's lap. Looking up at the old man and TE, for a moment it reflected the love that was about it. Yang lifted the large fish with both hands. 'May the chimes of your soul be the beauty and innocence that you are.'

Then TE leaned forward and gently took the fish from his master's hands and placed it back in the water. As it swam away, all the others flapped their tails together.

'That is the music of love. It is what we are.'

The lake became like a mirror, the ripples disappeared. And yet the bumboat glided through the water towards the side of the lake. Maybe it was the fish? Maybe it was the energy of the water? Or maybe it was the gift of the flame?

I am the learning

Sunflowers of Glass

The snow had been falling for three weeks, tiny snowflakes finally resting, finding their destination as a virgin white carpet, so pure, so serene. The lake became a frozen crystal embedded in the earth, reflecting its secrets of love and purity.

Yang's hut was cosy, the warmth from the wood stove saw to that. Both TE and Isinka had their special spaces. TE at the end of his master's bed and the little monkey in his hanging basket that Yang had made for his little friend. It was lined with soft cotton balls that Yang caught in the wind during the summer months. However, it was more often that Isinka would choose to sleep under Yang's beard – it was monkey Heaven there, closer to his master's heart.

Yang listened to the silence of the day. It reminded him of his being. Just then came a knock at the door. Yang opened a small space and could see the man's face.

'I am a traveller of many miles,' the man said. 'Do you have substance for my belly?'

Yang gave the traveller rice and fruit and a liquorice stick. The traveller thanked Yang, who blessed him and gave him the feather of trust.

The day passed as days do, into a night of dreams and nocturnal happiness. Early the following morning, just when the light showed its face, Yang heard the bark of a dog, then some tapping on his hut. Yang opened the small space in his door, so he could see the moment. The faces of two women presented themselves.

'It's the cold,' they said. 'It has got to us, can you help?'

Yang let them in – they were ready for the warmth and love. Even TE moved from his space and Isinka came down from his cosy to be next to these two cold souls. Yang gave them hot soup for their bellies. Just for a while they all sat together in complete harmony.

Yang smiled to himself. 'They have tasted the secret ingredient of my soup, and that is love.'

Soon it was time for them to go. Yang gave them both the green stone of compassion and a bag of food to take on their way. When they had left, he put more wood in the stove. The warmth was like the breath of a friend. Both his little friends had returned to their cosy places.

During the day Yang reflected on time and how he would never see it again, and that he could only feel it if he remembered. 'I must remember,' he kept saying. 'The key is to remember.' He looked in his store, the rice was getting low. He had given a good share to the travellers. The snow had covered his little hut completely, it looked like a white fairy cake, although Yang would never know what one of those was.

The days drifted like the snow, the breath of life danced slowly, beating hearts could be heard, sometimes together, sometimes apart, always singing the same songs of forgiveness. Yang's store looked less than little. He sang songs of wellbeing and tenderness to keep his spirits high, each day taking the flame into his heart, each day remembering.

A loud knock on his door awoke him from his dream of dreams. Yang opened the small space. He was looking at a large man with a black beard and grey eyes. 'The snow is deep, old man. I am lost – please give me a sign.'

'You must come in for a sign,' Yang replied.

So, the man, with others, cleared the snow away. He came into the hut and sat down.

'Look into your heart. What do you see?'

'Willingness and hope,' he answered.

'Is that all?' asked Yang.

The man thought. 'Love, understanding and peace,' he replied.

'So, you are not lost, my friend, for your heart will guide you.'

The man stood up. 'Thank you, old man.' He opened the door. 'Fill this friend's store,' he shouted to the others, 'so that he shall be joyous until the spring.' Soon Yang's store was overfull.

Yang thanked the man with the beard and grey eyes.

As he left, the man knelt at Yang's feet. 'Thank you. I am Prince Tunga, and you, sir, are the essence of my purpose.'

Yang blessed him, kissing his forehead. 'Be your heart and you shall never be lost.'

When the man had gone, Yang said a prayer of thanks. He sat in front of the warmth. TE, that bird with the silver wings and pink eyes, and Isinka, the complete happiness of life, joined him. For a moment they were in complete harmony – complete love.

Spirits love

Colour the Feeling

Yang lay under the mandarin tree. He was tired and needed sleep – it had been a busy morning, up early with the birds, tending to his garden and its vegetables. He lay down and closed his eyes then drifted into cloudland, where the white eagle soared above Yang's head as he approached the temple of spirits. It was a visit he made each year, when the water of the lake smiled no more and the jasmine fragrance was lost. It was his pilgrimage of awareness, returning home.

As he approached the temple, he could hear laughter and play. Yang frowned, for this was a sacred place, empty except for the gentle wind of grace.

Four men greeted him. 'Old man,' they said. 'You have come for nothing, for this is our place now, we have it for our fun.'

Yang could see they were taken with wine, their speech was mixed with badness. 'I ask you to leave now before the clouds throw darkness of your souls.'

'Old man,' one of them shouted. 'You are empty and of no meaning to us. Be off and take your shadow with you, for no-one will cry your empty space.'

Anger was now in Yang's heart, in his eyes. He threw off his cloak to reveal the black suit of the Master of Masters. Yang drew his sword, solid gold except for the Black Star. The men laughed, but just for a second as they realised the stranger no longer stood in front of them. Another moment later the largest bird they had ever seen flew out of the sky. It was silver with pink eyes, its talons of gold were as large as its body. On its back rode Yang, Master of Masters, warrior of warriors. Their smiles and their beings were never seen again. Many say they were turned into dust for the wind to scatter.

The great silver bird flew high in the sky, higher and higher. Yang the Master holding on, holding on until he felt himself slipping back, further and further. For a minute he was floating like a cloud, then falling and falling until he awoke under the mandarin tree, for it had all been a dream, a dream of darkness. Yang walked to his hut.

Both TE and Isinka sat inside, their eyes closed, their minds thinking alike. 'Let the flame return, let the consciousness return, let love rear its beautiful wings, let it fly.'

Yang lit a candle, his eyes searching the flame, searching for forgiveness for having such a dark dream. Later in front of a fire, he counted the stars. TE and Isinka joined him and together wished for peace and harmony, together they dreamt of love.

The following morning, the trees sang their song, the wind played its music ... Yang's heart felt sweet. 'For I have tasted, for I—'

His words were interrupted by four young men. 'Yang,' they spoke together, 'thank you, for we have learnt the way.' They each presented Yang with a small handful of dust.

Just for a moment his eyes diverted, then they had gone, the dust taken by the wind made its own way.

TE came and stood by his master. Isinka jumped on his shoulder. They turned towards the lake – it's reflection mirrored their love for each other.

We are blessed with peace

Why?

Yang walked in the fields. He went there to listen to the birds. 'I wonder what they are singing to each other,' he thought. 'Maybe they are asking questions or passing messages. Maybe they sing together creating harmony so that we beings can appreciate the love that is around us, the love we are?'

Just then, he came across a man beating his mule. 'Why do you hit your animal?' Yang asked.

'Because he is stubborn and won't do anything unless I take the stick to him.'

Yang took the stick from the man and threw it in the air, it went above the clouds. 'Your stick has now become truth.'

The man laughed. 'So, you can do tricks. Very funny.'

Yang leaned on his staff. 'So, what are you?' he asked.

'I am just a man,' he replied.

'Just? Tell me what is just? Can you read or write, can you be?'

A tear came to the man's eye as he lowered his head. 'No, I cannot do any of these things and it pains me inside.'

'How deep is that pain?' Yang asked, placing his hand on the man's forehead. 'Is it as painful as the stick on the mule's back? For that stick is the truth.'

Now the man was on his knees, his face buried in his hands. 'I feel shame,' he cried. 'I feel shame.'

Yang stood the man up and hugged him, then dried his eyes with his warm breath. 'Watch,' Yang said as he released the mule from its harness and plough. Yang then fed the animal some fruit from the garden of enlightenment. The animal ate with patience, occasionally stopping to thank Yang with its eyes.

When he had finished, Yang took the animal's head and held it close to his chest. The mule closed its eyes as Yang sang it a song. The words went something like this: 'Oh sacred one, you are true. For you are me as I am you. I am your pain from your past, for it has gone. It was the last.'

Yang then reconnected the animal to the harness and plough. 'Watch,' he said to the man and started to walk in front of the mule. It followed him, up and down the field.

Yang asked the man to do the same, and the mule followed him up and down the field. When they returned to Yang, he spoke to the man. 'You see you are not "just" for there is no such word. Take this bag. In it is wisdom and learning – there is everything, so now you can be.'

Yang walked on, occasionally turning around to watch the man, who often stopped to hug the mule's head.

Yang laughed. 'Love! It's so wonderful.'

As Yang continued on his way the birds sang in harmony, their song of love.

The pureness of honesty

Between Days

Yang awoke early, just as the sun was peeping, just as the birds were leaving their dreams behind. As he sat up, he gently held Isinka in his hands. The tiny creature, eyes closed, still in dreamtime. Yang lifted his little friend into his hanging basket, there he would continue to experience happiness, adventure, love.

The day was that of calm, serenity and gentleness. It was a Yang day. Yang walked towards the lake and sat on a large rock. With him was TE, his beautiful friend with the silver wings and pink eyes.

'My friend,' Yang asked. 'Show me what you need to know today.'

The large bird walked to the water's edge – its clearness was that of understanding, the reflection mirrored the knowing of himself. Just then he caught sight of the white fish with the turquoise eyes. For a moment both creatures connected with each other, there was a pure consciousness between them.

TE flapped his wings and took to the air, flying higher and higher. Yang stared at the magic, the gentleness, the wondrous gracefulness of his friend. Then just for a moment TE stopped, his body floating high above his master's head, then he instantly flew down to be next to the old man.

'Thank you my friend, for I know what to do.' Yang lay down on the earth and meditated. This took him into a state of awareness – he found his body lifting until it was above his physical body. He was having an out-of-body experience. For a moment all was still, the wind held its breath, the sound of life became a void, an empty space. Soon Yang returned, the clarity of his eyes was that of newborn crystals from Heaven.

Messages from Yang

'Thank you, TE, for now I know.' And yet as he spoke the words, he didn't have the answer.

Once again, TE walked to the edge of the lake – now its clearness was that of knowing the truth of love and the mirror of understanding the pure consciousness. Soon, the bird's body was contrasting against a yellow sky. The day had drifted slightly and yet silently, like thoughts on their never-ending journeys. Evening moths and others danced like raindrops of fire.

Yang was mesmerised by the magnificence of his silver friend. So serene, so pale. TE floated aimlessly above the skies, his wings still. Yang was in wonder – now he realised what he needed to do. After his friend had returned, Yang thanked him. 'Your beauty of the skies has taught me to be myself, as the day is the day, the night is the night, and the now is the knowing.'

Isinka joined them. Yang had enjoyed a day of finding out, now he wanted to be. Now the three of them sat watching the lake, its stillness and beauty were utter enchantment. They felt a pure love reflected back. Was it the serene beauty of life itself? Or the turquoise eyes of a friend that had been experiencing the moment?

Why live a lie?

Feathers of Happiness

Yang didn't know the name of the large shrub that stood not far from his hut. He was always going to ask a passing person, 'the next one maybe, or the next one.' The shrub never flowered and yet had a scent like Heaven. That's of course, if that place has a scent. Once again, the old man of consciousness was talking to himself, once again he was answering himself. When he did this, TE and Isinka sometimes had the look of bewilderment about them, that is, of bewilderment and love.

Today the shrub has three white feathers hanging from its branches, gently dancing, moving like the grace of the flame.

A man approached Yang. 'Please may I have a feather?' he asked.

'They are gifts,' Yang replied. 'Tell me what gift you are looking for?'

'I am looking for happiness.'

'Then take a feather, for you are the happiness.'

Soon a man with a woman came to Yang's place. 'Please,' they asked, 'may we have one of your feathers?'

'And what gift do you desire?'

'The gift of forgiveness.'

Yang gave them a feather. 'You are both forgiveness.'

Later in the day, a young boy came to Yang's hut. 'Excuse me, old man, but may I have that white feather?' he asked. 'I am making a coat of feathers for my mother; she is sick and unwell.'

Yang gave the boy the last white feather. 'Go home and place the feather next to your mother's bed. She will become well soon, for you have chosen the gift of love.'

'Does that mean that I have chosen you also, because you are love to have given me the feather?'

Yang smiled as he felt tenderness and grace for the boy. 'We are all love. The stars, the earth, the water, the breath of our souls. We are all love.'

The boy thanked Yang, kissed his hand, then left. That night, Yang, the Master of consciousness, the healer of lost souls, lay down to rest, for he was full of gratitude and peace. He was remembering his soul's purpose.

TE in the corner was remembering the messages his master had passed on, and little Isinka snuggled in Yang's beard, remembered his knowing. Just for a moment they were all remembering.

'Ah,' the old man sighed, '... remembering, it tastes so good. It tastes of love.'

Everything has choice

Messages

Messages

Messages

Messages

Messages

Messages

Messages

Messages